How shall we pray this morning?
For what shall we pray this night?

How shall we pray this morning?
For what shall we pray this night?

A month of worship resources
for a time of pandemic

Thom M Shuman

wild goose
publications

www.ionabooks.com

Copyright © Thom M Shuman
Published 2020 by
Wild Goose Publications
21 Carlton Court, Glasgow G5 9JP, UK,
the publishing division of the Iona Community.
Scottish Charity No. SC003794. Limited Company Reg. No. SC096243.

ISBN 978-1-84952-750-7

Cover images:
Barley field © kangbch, Sunset © Giani Pralea, both from Pixabay

The publishers gratefully acknowledge the support of the Drummond Trust, 3 Pitt Terrace, Stirling FK8 2EY in producing this book.

All rights reserved. Apart from the circumstances described below relating to non-commercial use, no part of this publication may be reproduced in any form or by any means, including photocopying or any information storage or retrieval system, without written permission from the publisher.

Non-commercial use:
The material in this book may be used non-commercially for worship and group work without written permission from the publisher. If photocopies of small sections are made, please make full acknowledgement of the source, and report usage to the CLA or other copyright organisation.

Thom M Shuman has asserted his right in accordance with the Copyright, Designs and Patents Act, 1988, to be identified as the author of this work.

Overseas distribution
Australia: Willow Connection Pty Ltd, Unit 4A, 3–9 Kenneth Road, Manly Vale, NSW 2093
New Zealand: Pleroma, Higginson Street, Otane 4170, Central Hawkes Bay

Printed by Bell & Bain, Thornliebank, Glasgow

How shall we pray this morning? For what shall we pray this night?

Contents

Introduction   7

Morning and evening prayer   9

Bible readings and poems for two weeks   123

Sources and acknowledgements   143

Introduction

When the Covid-19 pandemic began in winter/spring 2020, and we were forced to close down the church, I wanted to find a way to stay connected with my congregation and to continue worshipping together.

So I began to record a series of short videos of morning and evening prayers. As part of this offering, I would paraphrase or rework a psalm into a poetic piece which I called a canticle, as well as write a prayer that reflected what was happening in folk's lives, my life and the life of the world.

These short liturgies are some of the results of that effort, which continues during this time of uncertainty: of lockdown, partial lockdown, lockdown again, of adjusting to 'the new normal', of praying for effective treatments for Covid-19 and a vaccine …

If you would like to add Bible readings to the morning and evening worship, I suggest you do this between the canticle and the prayer. I use the daily lectionary of the Presbyterian Church here in the United States; I imagine your Church or community has something similar.

Most of the suggested songs and hymns are well-known and easy to find on the Internet; you might want to include others more familiar to you. You could sing the hymns, or speak the words like poetry. Words of well-loved songs and hymns can go very deep into the heart and soul.

The times are always changing, so please adapt these liturgies to your situation.

I've also included two weeks of Bible readings and poems. I hope this is helpful, and maybe inspires you to write your own poems and prayers based on lectionary readings. I've found the spiritual discipline of writing each day during this time very centring.

Grace and peace to you in the name of our Lord Jesus Christ.

Thom M Shuman,
Associate member of the Iona Community,
Columbus, Ohio, USA

Morning and evening prayer

MONDAY

Morning prayer

Opening:

Open our mouths, Precious God,
that we may speak your praises. Amen

Song: 'Joyful, joyful, we adore Thee' or 'In the Lord I'll be ever thankful' (Taizé)

Canticle:

I awake, my soul filled with
the ashes of faded dreams,
my throat as dry as sheets
hanging outside in the hot sun,
my hands as cracked as
the soil baked by 14 days
of a record-setting heatwave.

I edge out of bed and
walk down the hall looking for you,
and there you are
in the one room with an
overworked window fan,

12 *How shall we pray this morning? For what shall we pray this night?*

your face illuminated by
your gentle grace, as you
hold out your hands to
draw me onto your lap;
and as you share your
glass of iced tea glistening
with condensation, I snuggle
next to your heart, whispering
how much I love you.

Hand in hand, we walk to
the kitchen, and I sit
at the table watching you
busily mixing up a fresh
batch of biscuit dough.

And after my bath, as you help
me get dressed, you look me
in the eyes, reminding me that
the bullies have no power over me,
and that your hope is the
best friend anyone could have.

And as you hand me the sack lunch
(with two still-warm biscuits
dripping with butter and honey),
I give you a great, big bear hug
and walk down the sidewalk whistling.

Prayer:

How shall we pray this morning?

Do you ever wish you could pull the covers over your head,
Mothering God,
and snuggle back down into the warm bed without a care in the world?
We do. And these days, maybe more often than ever.
So, give us that little nudge, so we can put our feet out,
then our legs, stand and stretch, go to the window and look out,
and give thanks to you for this day we have been given:
to share hope, to create grace, to offer joy to others.

How shall we pray this morning?

Did you ever mutter from under the blanket, 'Just five more minutes',
Jesus our brother?
Surely you must have; we often do, in these days of uncertainty.
So, come and grab us by the hand, pulling us out of bed,
helping us to bathe and get dressed and face this day in which we can
walk with our God, simply by keeping an eye on others,
love the kindness offered to us by neighbours who drop off supplies,
and continue to do justice, even at a distance.

How shall we pray this morning?

Did you ever reach out and bash the alarm clock,
Spirit of our mornings,
grumbling under your breath, 'Who left that thing on?!'?
That's our response on a lot of mornings lately.

So, help us to wake up, not to a jangling alarm
but to the songs of joy you offer in these endless days,
to the whispers of wonder stirring the trees,
to the sound of healing echoing in hospital hallways.

How shall we pray this morning?

God of our mornings, of every morning,
wake us, walk with us, use us this day, we pray. Amen

Benediction:

And now, may the peace of the gentle breezes,
the peace of the singing birds,
the peace of the shining sun,
and the deep, deep peace of the Child of Peace
be with you.
Amen

Evening prayer

Opening:

O God, come to our assistance.
O God, we come into your presence this night. Amen

Song: 'Abide with me' or 'Be still and know' (John L Bell)

Canticle:

As we shelter in place,
may we find ourselves
in your backyard, lying in
the shade of old oaks
with our heads in your lap.

As we whisper, 'Our heart,
our home, our only hope,'
you grab our hands so we
don't step into fears' trap,
and chase away worry's hawk
as it swoops down to snatch us.

You tuck us in at night,
and wrap your arms tight around us.
If we awake with nightmares,
you whisper over and over, 'Don't be scared,'
and delete all the trolls' Tweets of the day
before we can pull them up on our devices.

16   How shall we pray this morning? For what shall we pray this night?

You are our comforter and strength,
and so, we curl up in your heart.
You are the light in our shadows,
our guide on this uncertain journey.

You place helpers all around us,
folk who do their best,
who comfort us when we are scared,
who take our temp when we are feverish,
who work around the clock to bring healing.

It is love which holds us together with you,
that love setting us free from terrors in our minds,
that love which wraps us in your sheltering grace.

We call, we cry, we shout, we whisper in total trust,
knowing you lift us up, carry us in your arms of hope,
reminding us over and over, 'I am still here, always,'
blessing us with life even in the dimmest moments,
blessing us with life even in the days of doubt,
blessing us with life, even beyond the end of time.

Prayer:

For what shall we pray this night?

We come to you this night, O God,
with sighs too deep for words,
with worries we cannot share with anyone else,
with fears that lodge just outside our memories:
hear us this night, we pray …

For what shall we pray this night?

We come to you this night, Jesus of the mysteries,
with questions that race around our minds,
with hopes that we dare not whisper,
with love that seems to be dimming:
hear us this night, we pray …

For what shall we pray this night?

We come to you this night, Spirit of gentleness,
with hearts worn out from racing around during the day,
with bodies fatigued by too many tasks,
with souls frazzled by boredom that wraps around us.
Hear us this night, we pray,
as in the silence, we offer the prayers of our hearts …

Silence

Be in our hearts this night, God, Jesus, Spirit,
Holy and One. Amen

Benediction:

And now, may the peace of the rolling waves,
the peace of the silent mountains,
the peace of the singing stars,
and the deep, deep peace of the Prince of Peace
be with you.
Amen

TUESDAY

Morning prayer

Opening:

O God, as we come into your presence,
may our songs fill your heart. Amen

Song: 'Morning has broken' or 'Halle, halle, halle' (Caribbean)

Canticle:

The smoky-voiced
scat singer
backed by the overly enthusiastic
handbell ringer,
producing a psalm.

The hobo on the oboe,
the buffoon with the bassoon,
with bling-burdened rappers
and street-corner finger-snappers,
all shape notes into spirituals.

The organ grinder's monkey
dancing for a dime,

and the fourth-grader
mastering ragtime,
orchestrate an oratorio,
with the mountains taking
the low notes
and the stars the descant.

New songs
composed in your heart,
Ghostwriter of joy,
and planted deep in our souls,
just waiting to burst forth –
a flood of praise!

Prayer:

How shall we pray this morning?

What will this day bring, O God? We don't have a clue!
But you are not only the author of the mystery of life,
you are that very mystery itself:
for your beauty does not reside in the heavens
but is among us in the bluejays on our lawns,
the pear trees blossoming in our backyards,
the hawks circling in the sky.
May we be a part of your mystery this day.

How shall we pray this morning?

20 *How shall we pray this morning? For what shall we pray this night?*

What will happen during this day, Brother Jesus, we wonder.
We could wallow in loneliness – show us how to care for others.
We could think only of ourselves – teach us new songs
to sing to our neighbours.
We could sit, and sit, and sit – help us to get up and move:
yoga on television, a walk around the neighbourhood,
a bouncy dance with our grandkids,
a good, long stretching routine.

How shall we pray this morning?

What will we hear this day, Breath of our life?
Will we focus on the wanderings of politicians
or listen to the whisper of the breezes?
Will we hear the anger, the fear, the worries offered endlessly
or the songs of your heart offering trust and grace.
Will we simply stuff our ears with the cotton of uncertainty
or open ourselves up to every word of hope, of love, of life?

How shall we pray this morning?

Walk with us this day, O God,
so we may discover our part in the mystery,
share the wonder of life
and listen to your heart in every moment. Amen

Benediction:

And now, may the peace of the gentle breezes,
the peace of the singing birds,
the peace of the shining sun,
and the deep, deep peace of the Child of Peace
be with you.
Amen

Evening prayer

Opening:

In the quiet, we come to you, O God;
listen to our hearts in these moments. Amen

Song: 'Day is done but love unfailing' or 'Come, bring your burdens to God' (South Africa)

Canticle:

As I lie in the shadows,
you are my night light,
and I am not afraid of
monsters under the bed
or in the closet's corner.
When I am running from
my worst fears, you gather
me up in your safe arms.

My longing to be in your presence
is so deep I can almost taste it;
I desire to wander through
the rooms of your heart,
to discover all your delights
and to sit with a nice cup of tea
as you answer the long list of questions
I have carried for so many years.

When despair stalks me in every moment,
you take me by the hand and
place me in hope's playroom
where we can spend days in peace.

Surrounded by those who don't
know me or care for me, I look over
their heads and see you coming,
and I begin to sing the songs of joy
the Spirit taught me so long ago.

I whisper, I croak, I shout,
and you hear me, answering
with the invitation to come
and simply sit with you
on the front porch in that
still, small silence of grace.

You never push me away
but draw me closer.
You will not toss me aside
in the bin of disrepute.
Even if my family locks me out,
you open wide the door
of your heart to me.

When I stumble from pothole
to pothole, you grab my hand
to teach me how to skip down
the sidewalks of your neighbourhood.

24   How shall we pray this morning? For what shall we pray this night?

You will not let the liars or the haters
have the final word about me.

In every moment, through every shadow,
in the little child sharing a sandwich,
in the retiree mentoring a student,
in the nurse holding the hand of a patient,
in the prisoner raising a service dog,
your goodness breaks forth into sight.

Give me the patience to simply wait,
gracious God,
for your joy, your wonder, your peace,
your hope, your grace, your love,

to simply wait in faith.

Prayer:

For what shall we pray this night?

O God, let your children now go in peace
into your comforting arms;
your word of gentleness, of being present with us,
of cradling us in your heart has come true.

For what shall we pray this night?

O Jesus, we have seen the hope you bring to us:
in the kindness of those who reached out to us,
in the virtual arms of those who love us,
in the strangers who unexpectedly cared for us.

For what shall we pray this night?

O Spirit, we have seen your Light,
in the stuffed animals and rainbows on porches and in windows,
in the unsigned notes of encouragement in our mailboxes,
in those coming up with new kinds of masks and gowns and tests.

For what shall we pray this night?

God, Jesus, Spirit,
who is, who was, who shall be,
we have seen you watching over us. Amen

Benediction:

And now, may the peace of the rolling waves,
the peace of the silent mountains,
the peace of the singing stars,
and the deep, deep peace of the Prince of Peace
be with you.
Amen

WEDNESDAY

Morning prayer

Opening:

As we begin this day in quiet, God,
may we be graced by your love. Amen

Song: 'Cantemos al Señor' or 'If you believe and I believe' (Zimbabwe)

Canticle:

Sometimes, creation scares us –
with mighty thunderstorms,
raging and flooding rivers,
winds that bend the trees
until they almost break.

Sometimes, creation sings
lullabies to us, with soft
breezes that stir the curtains
on sweltering summer nights.

Sometimes, creation stuns
with brilliant full moons that fill the sky,
meteors chasing one another,
the sun that blinds our eyes.

So many wonders, so many ways
in which we hear you holler, whisper,
speak, sing to us through
the gift of your imagination all around us.

Sometimes, your words scare us –
when you thunder about
how justice should be like a
raging, flooding river of hope,
washing away the mistreatment
of your beloved children.

Sometimes, your words are love songs,
composed in the quiet
of your heart, played gently on
an acoustic guitar, which we hear
when we settle down our souls
and are willing to listen.

Sometimes, your words are
simple invitations: to follow that
itinerant teacher with no credentials,
to attend parties with scoundrels,
to forgive those who hurt our feelings.

So many words, so many stories,
in which we hear you holler, whisper,
speak, sing to us through
the gift of your imagination all around us.

May our imagination delight you,
may our words sing to you,

may our lives reflect you, our God,
your strength, your hope, your love.

Prayer:

How shall we pray this morning?

Before we woke up, Watchful God,
you were in the kitchen
fixing breakfast for truck drivers hitting the road,
making sandwiches for those who will be clerking in stores,
filling up thermoses with coffee and tea for the home-delivery folk.
May we do something to remember and thank them this day.

How shall we pray this morning?

Before we crawled out of bed, Jesus of justice,
you were setting up tables on corners to feed the hungry,
sewing face masks for those on the frontlines of caring,
meeting with policymakers to ensure healthcare for the most vulnerable.
May we do something to help those in need this day,
even from the sanctuaries of our homes.

How shall we pray this morning?

While we were in the shower, Spirit of hope,
you were patiently showing a parent the intricacies of 5th-grade math,
holding up a too-weary-for-words night nurse in an ICU unit,
standing by the chaplain offering a prayer at a graveside
where no family members were allowed.
May we find a way to care for those overwhelmed by this 'new normal'.

How shall we pray this morning?

While we are just starting our day,
God in Community, Holy and One,
you have already been up, and busy,
and just waiting for us to jump in to help,
even, and especially,
when we think there is nothing we can do. Amen

Benediction:

And now, may the peace of the gentle breezes,
the peace of the singing birds,
the peace of the shining sun,
and the deep, deep peace of the Child of Peace
be with you.
Amen

Evening prayer

Opening:

May we rest in your grace this night, O God,
as you sing us lullabies. Amen

Song: 'All praise to Thee, my God, this night' or 'I waited patiently for God'
(John L Bell)

Canticle:

Help us to break free
from the bondage of
fear's isolation, so we may
learn a new language,
based on hope not hubris,
on caring not sarcasm,
on love not injustice.

Then folk will know that
we are God's safe faith space,
the home where all are welcome;

then the tsunami of taunts
will become a toddlers' pool
for wading and splashing;

then the rivers in valleys
will wash away the sludge

of despair running down
the mountains of monotony;

then the earth will quiver like
a tuning fork, as choirs
prepare to sing glad songs of joy
to the One who turns
loneliness into neighbourhoods of hope –

who shatters frozen hearts
so they can melt into cups
of grace offered to everyone.

Prayer:

For what shall we pray this night?

Parenting God, we pray for all whose dreams
have turned to ashes even before they woke up:
for high school and university students
who thought they would be walking across stages
before proud families and friends;
for those who looked forward to competing in sports events
they had been training for over months and years;
for all who had planned trips to celebrate their spring break,
their retirement …

For what shall we pray this night?

Jesus of the vulnerable, we pray for those
who are not the privileged of the world:

for those who were furloughed for a few weeks
which is now stretching into months;
for those who wonder how they will be able
to pay for a simple trip to the doctor,
much less a hospital stay fighting a virus;
for those who will sit in a traffic jam for hours
just to get a box of food which is supposed
to last for a week or ten days.

For what shall we pray this night?

Spirit of the loving God,
we pray for those whose days are filled with endless worries:
for those who cannot afford to buy a tank of gas
in a time of the lowest petrol prices in decades;
for those whose mailboxes are stuffed with flyers
for things they can't begin to imagine, but
no cards from friends, no letters from family;
for those who will slip under the covers with loneliness.

For what shall we pray this night?

God in Community, Holy and One, we pray this night,
as we have every night for so long,
that sleep will come home and curl up next to us,
that our dreams will be filled with hope and not horrors,
that the long hours we fear will turn out to be just fleeting moments
before we drift off into the grace and comfort of your heart. Amen

Benediction:

And now, may the peace of the rolling waves,
the peace of the silent mountains,
the peace of the singing stars,
and the deep, deep peace of the Prince of Peace
be with you.
Amen

THURSDAY

Morning prayer

Opening:

We come to you in these moments, Gracious God,
so that we can walk in your grace this day. Amen

Song: 'Holy, Holy, Holy! Lord God Almighty!' or 'God to enfold you' (John L Bell and Graham Maule)

Canticle:

Like a kitten stretching
for a toy under the dresser,
I reach out for your hand.
Like a dog running to the water bowl
after a long walk,
I am parched for your grace.
Where can I go
to be able to look you
in the eyes?
I hang out my salty, wet
sheets in the morning,
while my neighbours whisper,

'Have you seen God
any time this week?'

Deeper than any echo,
I recall walking to church
with my family,
going to sing glad songs,
learn stories about you,
share our lives and hopes.
Why are you so mopey,
Spirit deep within me,
and why are you
so vexed over me?
I will wait on you,
my rescuer, my God,
so I can sing
your glad songs again.

Deep down, I seem
at loose ends, and
so I recall those thin places
where I found you.

In the waterfalls in mountains,
in eddies of pools,
in the waves on the shore,
I am baptised in your waters.

Each morning,
you pack a lunch
filled with love

to strengthen me.
When you look at the photos
on top of your bureau,
is mine hidden behind others?
I shuffle down pity's path
while bullies torment me.
I ache deep inside my bones,
while neighbours whisper,
'So have you seen God recently?'

Why are you down in the dumps,
Spirit which is my companion,
and why do you
pester me so much?
I need to find you, O God,
so I can once again
sing praises to you.

Prayer:

How shall we pray this morning?

It's getting harder and harder to get out
of bed each morning, O God,
so, help us to smell the coffee of hope
you are brewing in the kitchen, so we can
pour a cup and share it (virtually) with a friend
over the phone, or Skype or FaceTime,
so we do not miss the sunrise of wonder
you are putting into our souls.

How shall we pray this morning?

It's getting harder and harder to care for others
each, and every, day, Jesus of the forgotten,
as we worry if we have enough for however long this lasts.
So, hand us a box to fill with that food we are hoarding,
to set on a neighbour's porch.
Give us the address of that lonely couple across town,
so that we can send them a card to remind them (and us)
that justice can be as simple as
reaching out to the stranger.

How shall we pray this morning?

It's getting harder and harder to muster any energy
these days, Spirit of life,
so stand us under the shower
of your peace, your joy, your grace, your kindness
so we can begin to sing a morning song, not a dirge,
so we can recall the good things we have, and not dwell on the negative,
so we can notice your beloved out delivering groceries
and medication and hope and offer them
a wave, a smile, a thank you, a generous gift, our hearts.

How shall we pray this morning?

It's getting harder and harder, God in Community, Holy and One,
so we pray that we can find energy, grace, wonder
and hope from you,
so that we live each day
as your people of faith, justice and caring. Amen

38 How shall we pray this morning? For what shall we pray this night?

Benediction:

And now, may the peace of the gentle breezes,
the peace of the singing birds,
the peace of the shining sun,
and the deep, deep peace of the Child of Peace
be with you.
Amen

Evening prayer

Opening:

As we settle down from this day, O God,
may we be cradled in your grace. Amen

Song: 'Now the day is over' or 'Peace I leave with you'

Canticle:

I can easily sing
after tripping over my faults,
as you pick me up
and bandage my scraped knees.
You throw down a hope ladder
to help me climb out of the blues,
and so I join the a cappella group
beat-boxing your name.
Your pique withers, your ill humour fades
but your grace is never withdrawn.
My heart breaks in the night,
but Joy tiptoes in to wake me up in the morning.

On those bright, sunny,
all-is-well-with-the-world days,
nothing will bother me.

You hiked with me to watch
the sun rise over the mountains,
then you ran down the hill

out of my sight,
and I could not find the path.
I yelled for help, wondering
'Who's going to rejoice
if there is no one to hear?
Does dusty death know your songs?
Will the grave shout your name?
If you can hear me, reach out
and show me the way!'

Then, I will shuck open grief
and find joy's pearl;
I will slip out of my hair shirt
and put on your wonder,
singing to you, not just
on those bright, sunny,
all-is-well-with-the-world days,
but on all my Eeyore ones
as well.

Prayer:

For what shall we pray this night?

We often find ourselves in the shadows of uncertainty,
God of moons and stars,
so may the light of your presence be with us this night.

For what shall we pray this night?

As we settle down, plump our pillows,
Jesus our Brother;
as we stretch and yawn, whisper into our hearts;
as we drift into sleep, keep watch over us, we pray.

For what shall we pray this night?

Your peace surrounds us in these moments of rest,
Spirit of gentleness;
your grace fills our dreams with comfort and peace;
your arms hold us so we know we are safe.

For what shall we pray this night?

Until we wake in the morning,
God in Community, Holy and One,
shelter us in your love, your grace, your peace. Amen

Benediction:

And now, may the peace of the rolling waves,
the peace of the silent mountains,
the peace of the singing stars,
and the deep, deep peace of the Prince of Peace
be with you.
Amen

FRIDAY

Morning prayer

Opening:

As we prepare to set out on this day's journey,
may we spend a few moments in your grace, O God. Amen

Song: 'Arise, your light is come' or 'Take, O take me as I am' (John L Bell)

Canticle:

Your grace is as close
as every breath we take;
your love clings tighter to us
than any Velcro fastener;
and so we tell everyone
of how you reach out
and gather us from
every edge to which we wander.

Some arrive at the edge,
social distancing,
weary and broken,
hungering for hope,
thirsting for just a sip
of friendship, of a 'hello'.

Some huddle in shadowed doorways,
sleep rough in parks,
listening to the well-off
use words like 'short-term' and
'coming back better than ever'.
They had worked hard all their lives,
but furloughed, and told to wait a while,
lost everything, especially dignity.

They cried to God, who
brings light into the dimmest corners,
who shatters despair with hope,
who puts them to work sharing grace
with those who know they have enough,
singing of the One who has never used
the word hopeless about anyone.

Some became addicted to scams,
offered by those seeking
to increase their bank accounts;
while others lie awake searching
the Internet for easy cures.

They cried to God, who
offers love's brokenness
and wraps them in bands of compassion
soaked with the tears of grace,
and they run to tell others
of the One who will shelter them
in welcome and kindness.

Some are buffeted by angry words,
tossed about on the seas of bitterness,
set adrift by those filled with hate.
They knew the love of God,
the hope God has for all,
but the waves of vilification and judgement
tossed them far into the air,
and sank them into rejection's depths.

Finally, when it seemed even Hope
had abandoned all hope,
they cried to God, who
told the Tweeters to be still,
and the trolls to shut their mouths.
In the quiet of God's heart
they found their true home,
joining their sisters and brothers
and all their mentors and models in faith
in shouts of acclamation.

For there is One who
will turn floods of vitriol
into dusty dry riverbanks,
who will let hate's wine
become bitter vinegar poured
into the cups of those who
turn their backs on others.

And he turns food deserts
into farmers' markets for the starving;

he fixes the broken pipes so grace
flows without ceasing;

he teaches the hungry the best recipes,
and settles them into
neighbourhoods of hope
where they can plant community gardens
and put fresh produce
on each other's porches,
blessing others as deeply
as God has blessed them.

But those who think they are
holier than others are put in their place,
sent into timeout until they relearn
the ABCs of love's language.
And the vulnerable?
They become God's trusted council,
grace's children applauding with joy,
while the despots lose their voices.

If we have any smarts at all,
we will pay more attention
to God's faithful love.

Prayer:

How shall we pray this morning?

Though we are still dealing with increasing
numbers of cases and deaths,
though the scientists and medical folk
are still concerned about new waves,
though there are so many, oh so many,
out of work, struggling to make ends meet,
yet, we will give you thanks this Friday morning, O God:

for those who, despite their overwhelming weariness,
still go in for another shift at the hospital;
for those who still don't have all the pieces,
but are beginning to put together the puzzle of a vaccine;
for those who refuse to let their employees
return to work in unsafe conditions yet continue to pay them.

How shall we pray this morning?

Though we continue to see evidence every day
that the pandemic of hate, violence and fear has not abated,
though the angriest of voices, the loudest of voices,
continue to dominate the news cycle on every media,
though the most vulnerable continue to shoulder
the burden of the heaviest risks of this virus,
yet, we will give you thanks this morning, Jesus our Companion:

for those who continue to work in care facilities,
because hope and compassion are needed there;
for those who sit on the sidewalk and lawn of their neighbours
to be a friendship-barrier protecting them from anger;
for those who are putting together boxes of supplies
and delivering them to those who have nothing.

How shall we pray this morning?

Though we get up in the morning and wonder
whether or not kindness might be featured on the news,
though we walk through the day, through these long days,
looking for glimpses of grace in the flurries of fear,
though we come to each evening realising that

the folk who don't know much have too much to say,
yet, we will give you thanks this morning, Spirit of our lives:

for those who choose to spend the morning
caring for those who have no one to look after them;
for those who risk leaving the safety of their homes
to pick up groceries for the single mum;
for those who write new songs of grace,
who compose cantatas of compassion,
who tell new stories to scared kids.

How shall we pray this morning?

Though every day seems like an endless Monday of
fears, worries, fatigue, hopelessness, grumpiness,
yet, we will give you thanks this morning,
God in Community, Holy and One,
because you have not forgotten us,
you have not abandoned us,
you are always with us. Amen

Benediction:

And now, may the peace of the gentle breezes,
the peace of the singing birds,
the peace of the shining sun,
and the deep, deep peace of the Child of Peace
be with you.
Amen

Evening prayer

Opening:

In the stillness of this night, O God,
may we hear your songs of gentleness. Amen

Song: 'God of our life' or 'Don't be afraid' (John L Bell)

Canticle:

Shout for joy to God!

Everyone, everywhere,
every nation, every language,
every planet, every galaxy
throughout all creation –
shout for joy to God!

For God's love is not
just never-ending –
it is ever-sending.

God does not just say
that we are never alone –
but like a child's Velcro dog,
God never leaves our side,
ever, never!

Shout for joy to God!

Prayer:

For what shall we pray this night?

Like the disciples in that upper room so long ago,
loving God, we find ourselves isolated from the world,
the windows of our souls shuttered, the doors to our hearts locked,
wondering who or what and when something will come and get us.

So, in our terror, touch us with your presence;
as our hearts tremble, calm us with a touch;
in our frightened silence, speak to us of hope and grace.

For what shall we pray this night?

Like your friends in the shadowed room so long ago,
Jesus of the empty tomb, we find ourselves
clasping our selves trying to stop the shaking,
afraid of what might be lurking just outside the edge of our worries,
and questioning whether you really care for us.

For what shall we pray this night?

Like those who found courage in that room so long ago,
Spirit of strength, we wonder if we can step forward in faith,

to confess our fears and uncertainties,
to reach out and greet the One who is scarred for us,
to be willing to say, without a shred of evidence, 'Our Lord, our God.'

So, come in these moments of questioning,
to breathe courage,
to whisper our names,

50 How shall we pray this morning? For what shall we pray this night?

to fill us with the sweet breath
of hope, of wonder, of trust, of love,
of belief.

For what shall we pray this night?

Like you came to those in that room so long ago,
come in these evening moments
and fill us with you,
God in Community, Holy and One. Amen

Benediction:

And now, may the peace of the rolling waves,
the peace of the silent mountains,
the peace of the singing stars,
and the deep, deep peace of the Prince of Peace
be with you.
Amen

SATURDAY

Morning prayer

Opening:

Early in the morning, we come to find you, O God,
knowing you are already waiting for us. Amen

Song: 'Lord of all hopefulness' or 'Lord of Life, we come to you'

Canticle:

Our souls rejoice in you,
God of wonder and grace!

The words of politicians –
be they right wing,
left wing, or wingless –
so often turn to dust
(just as they do); their
plans drift away like chaff.

Our hope is in you,
God of our faith;
hope which comes
not only once a year on a holy night,
but is ours in every breath we take,

a gift from the One who
flung galaxies into the heavens,
who never breaks a promise,
who lifts the forgotten to their feet,
who places extra chairs around the dinner table
until everyone has a place.

God picks the locks on
every fear and anger
which imprisons us.

God tilts our heads up
from our devices, so
we can see the needy.

God teaches us justice
as the basic skill we need.

God keeps an eye on those
we have turned our backs on.

God cradles the lonely mourners,
and sits in doorways with kids
who have been locked out
of the homes they grew up in.

God holds each of us accountable
for how we treat the vulnerable.

God's love, hope, grace, peace,
wonder, joy, welcome never become
obsolete.

Our souls rejoice in you,
God of grace and wonder!

Prayer:

How shall we pray this morning?

It is another day when we feel like we're trapped
in the maze from *Harry Potter and the Goblet of Fire*;
another day where we wander around and around,
everything looking the same
whatever direction we look,
and we wonder if we will ever get out,
or just end up forgotten.

So, come to us this day, to take us by the hand.
Lead us from point A to point B
by the most direct path, Holy God,
so we know we can find our way out.

How shall we pray this morning?

It is another day when we feel like we're trapped
in one of those escape rooms,
and it doesn't matter how creative we are, how smart,
how long or hard we work at trying to solve the puzzles which
will allow us to unlock the door –
we just cannot seem to do it.
And we wait for the Game guide
to at least press the button to let us out of this room of isolation;

and when nothing happens, suddenly Jesus, who has been
standing in the corner all the time,
pats his pocket and pulling out the key,
unlocks the door and ushers us back out into hope.

How shall we pray this morning?

It is another day where we find ourselves like that mythical character.
Oh, who was it? Sisyphus!
We are pushing that great big rock of uncertainty up the hill,
straining and shoving and nudging it bit by bit by bit,
until just as we are almost at the top, it suddenly rocks back and
begins to roll back down the hill again while we chase after it …

until, at the very bottom, we see you, Spirit of surprises,
standing with a sledgehammer, and with a few mighty whacks,
you crumble the rock into a pile of pebbles,
and giving each of us a handful, you say,
'If we each do our small part, we will get the big job done.'

How shall we pray this morning?

It is another day, God in Community, Holy and One,
so remind us that as long as you are with us,
we are not trapped, not locked in,
not given a task we cannot complete. Amen

Benediction:

And now, may the peace of the gentle breezes,
the peace of the singing birds,
the peace of the shining sun,
and the deep, deep peace of the Child of Peace
be with you.
Amen

Evening prayer

Opening:

In the silence, in the stillness, come, God,
to quiet our souls and warm our hearts. Amen

Song: 'Be still my soul' or 'In God alone' (Taizé)

Canticle:

They have been chasing us
all day long, loving God:
our fears, our worries, our questions,
longing to snip us into little pieces
with their sharpened scissors of doubt
or drag us into their traps;
so we long to climb up into your lap
where we know we are safe.

We know how easy it is to just
slow down and let them catch us,
to give up and fall into their hands,
but you keep pressing us to keep moving,
to not give up.

You get as annoyed as we do
by their persistence in trying
to seduce us away from you,
and you surround us, even at a distance,
with those who model that faithful trust in you for us to emulate.

So may we be found joining them
in keeping faith in you, with you.
One day, in your good time,
the unfriendly folk will lose their power,
as you surround us with the strength
which is found in the weakness of compassion,
and with the courage that can be found
in caring for others more than ourselves.

So, when you get ready to look around
to see who is sharing your grace,
offering your peace, caring for the vulnerable,
living out the gospel of justice and hope,
we pray that we will be found in that group
which is doing exactly all those things.

Because, when we live such lives,
when we offer our hearts, our hands,
our hopes, our lives to others,
we are indeed not just singing about you
but showing others who you are.

Prayer:

For what shall we pray this night?

So many are talking about how much better life will be
in the months and years to come,
yet you know, God of all people, those who
will not experience better, newer, wealthier, healthier.
Those whose jobs, if they are still there, will continue

to be the lowest paid, with no benefits, no healthcare.
Those who gave up looking for work long before this crisis
because they are 'too old', have been out of work for too long, whatever.
Those homeless, hungry, lonely, ignored,
whose lives will not change, no matter what anyone says.

Lord, hear our prayer …

For what shall we pray this night?

There are those who claim that cases are going up
simply because the number of tests has increased,
yet you know, Jesus of the caregivers, all those
nurses, doctors, paramedics, first responders,
clerks in stores, cooks, delivery drivers, caregivers
seeing the reality of what is happening due
to our eagerness to go to bars and parties
and crowd in at beaches,
rather than still being cautious, still being aware.

Lord, hear our prayer …

For what shall we pray this night?

Well, folk said that communities should just reopen –
everything – schools, stores, restaurants, churches –
that we don't need to wear masks, or stay at home, or at a distance,
yet you know those who still cannot visit their grandparents in care homes,
Spirit of the heartbroken,
those who will not be able to travel this summer,
those who are not allowed to come and tell family of their love,
those who cannot gather for funerals,

those who wonder if they will ever be able to
sing in the chorus again.

Lord, hear our prayer ...

For what shall we pray this night?

This night, God, Jesus, Spirit, we pray for all
who know the reality of these days, these times,
far better than all those who don't have a clue
what they are bringing forth. Amen

Benediction:

And now, may the peace of the rolling waves,
the peace of the silent mountains,
the peace of the singing stars,
and the deep, deep peace of the Prince of Peace
be with you.
Amen

SUNDAY

Morning prayer

Opening:

We praise you early in the morning, God of love,
our glad songs rising to welcome you. Amen

Song: 'When morning gilds the skies' or 'Bless the Lord' (Taizé)

Canticle:

No single word describes you,
Holiness of our hearts:
you sit on the floor playing jacks;
you walk the sidelines
as we run up and down creation's pitch;
you could boss us around,
but chose to learn how to crawl
on your hands and knees just like us;
you join in the silly jingles
we make up to give you thanks.

You gave visions to Jeremiah
and spoke to Elijah in a still, small voice.

You taught Miriam how to dance
and sang backup for Hannah and Mary.
You listened to every voice,
every heartbreak, every hope
from those in Eden to this very moment.
On mountaintops and in clouds,
cooking breakfast on a beach
and sleeping in the back of a boat,
you taught us your dreams;
you showed us how to care for others.

You lean over to hear our souls;
you wipe every mistake we make
off the whiteboard of life.
You step between us
and the bullies who would taunt us until
we turn and run.

We sing your praises over and over –
in churches and on playgrounds,
in grocery stores and classrooms,
in museums and malls, on boats and bicycles,
for wherever we are, everywhere we are,
we are standing on holy ground,
holding your hand tight.

Prayer:

How shall we pray this morning?

It has reached the point, God of all time,
when we are not even sure what day it is:
Monday, Thursday, Saturday – they are all the same.
If it was not for our devices,
or even that antiquated standby, the newspaper,
we might never know.
Remind us that this is not only the day you made,
but is your day – filled with wonder,
with creation putting on a show for us.

How shall we pray this morning?

Lord of holy and unholy moments, what day is it?
Is it another day when we will be so focused on our to-do lists
that we ignore the moments we are given to simply be –
in silence, in peace, in grace – in your presence?
Is it just another day when we are too busy to notice the vulnerable,
or will you open our eyes to those simple ways in which
we can be justice for all those who are ignored?

How shall we pray this morning?

Spirit of fleeting seconds,
come into our lives to shake us out of our lethargy
and these monotonous routines that have become 'the new normal':

Be that wet-nosed dog nudging us out of bed to go chase squirrels;
be that little kid who has messed up the kitchen

trying to make pancakes, serving us breakfast in bed;
be that cat rubbing up against our legs, until we pick you up
and hear you purring peace against us, and just want
to sit with you in our lap all day long.

How shall we pray this morning?

What day is it, God in Community, Holy and One?
It is *your* day – and we are overjoyed that you
will spend your day with us. Amen

Benediction:

And now, may the peace of the gentle breezes,
the peace of the singing birds,
the peace of the shining sun,
and the deep, deep peace of the Child of Peace
be with you.
Amen

Evening prayer

Opening:

Now, in the quiet, now, in the gentleness,
may we prepare to rest in your grace, O God. Amen

Song: 'Come down, O Love Divine' or 'O Lord, hear my prayer' (Taizé)

Canticle:

Let this be our grace
at each meal:
God's love feeds us always.

Let this be our song
throughout the day:
God's love is the music we need.

Let this be our praise
with every breath we take:
God's love sustains us.

In the rain dripping off trees,
in the stars twinkling at night,
in the mist over the ponds,
in the aurora borealis in the sky,
and the freshness of the evening,
we discover creation's affirmation:
God's love is forever.

Those set free from slavery's grip
in Egypt, Britain, the United States …

those who have passed through
the deep waters of hurricanes;

those who defeated fascism
and established justice for the vulnerable;

those who share from their abundance,
and the poor who give from the bottom of their hearts,
all declare the same truth:

God's love is stronger than evil.

The ones the world forgets,
but who are never abandoned by God;

those who are tossed aside by the cruel,
but are given new life by God;

those who empty out their pantries,
and those who fill the loneliness of neighbours,
all testify to what has always been known:

God's love never runs out.
God's love is infinite.
God's love is poured out over and over,
simply because God loves us,
all of us.

Prayer:

For what shall we pray this night?

Let us pray for all who are making decisions that affect others:
for those who are planning on opening communities and countries.
We pray for wisdom, compassion and caution
to be parts of these discussions, these decisions
that will affect so many in the days and weeks to come.
We pray for your patience, God of time, to rest upon all
who are involved in such matters.

For what shall we pray this night?

Let us pray for those for whom the coming week seems so familiar,
with isolation, with trying to find new books to read,
new activities to fill the seemingly endless hours.
We pray for those who are longing to go back to work,
who wonder not only when that might happen,
but what it might look like, and who worry about
safety, distancing and health.
We pray for your presence to surround them, Companion of our lives,
in these moments and the coming days.

For what shall we pray this night?

Let us pray for all who continue to be overwhelmed
by the uncertainty of these days:
persons with cognitive disabilities who cannot understand
why their lives and routines have been overturned,
those who long to have children and grandchildren run into their arms,
but can only wave to them through windows.

66 How shall we pray this morning? For what shall we pray this night?

For what shall we pray this night?

We pray for sleep to cradle us in the night,
God of love,
and for patience to be the sun's companion in the morning.

We pray for hope to come and curl up next to us in bed,
Jesus of our emptiness,
and to gently waken us with its whiskers in the morning.

We pray for peace to be the night light shining in the hallway,
Spirit of the resurrection,
so if we wake up in the middle of the night,
we can find our way to you,
God in Community, Holy and One. Amen

Benediction:

And now, may the peace of the rolling waves,
the peace of the silent mountains,
the peace of the singing stars,
and the deep, deep peace of the Prince of Peace
be with you.
Amen

MONDAY

Morning prayer

Opening:

Now, at the beginning of this day, of this week,
we seek your love to fill us in these moments, God of our lives. Amen

Song: 'Awake, my soul, and with the sun' or 'He came down' (Cameroon)

Canticle:

I wake up, and
there they are,
all my old friends, worries
and fears, walking
around and yelling their heads off,
telling me on all the media
that the only hope
I (we) have in these days
is in them and their anger,
their threats, their fears,
not in silly, old, compassionate
you.

68   How shall we pray this morning? For what shall we pray this night?

But you hold the robe
of hope for us to slip
our arms into; you sit
across the table, cradling
your cup of coffee, your heart
wide open to listen to us.

We fell asleep in your
comforting arms and grace;
we wake up again, and
you feed us with wonder,
joy, peace and gentleness.
So what if they have surrounded
the house, chanting and yelling
all their dire warnings of
how dumb we are to shelter,
to stay safe, to care for others.

You woke up way before
we did (if you ever dozed off)
and are ready to walk
by our side, between us
and all the bullies who
point and taunt us for
trusting in you rather than in
their ways.

You are the One who cares
for us more than anyone;
we will care enough to share
your blessings this day.

Prayer:

How shall we pray this morning?

It is Monday, God of this day, but then
every day seems like a Monday now:
the day when we don't want to get up,
the day when we don't want to think about
what lies ahead,
the day when we wonder where the weekend went.

How shall we pray this morning?

It is Monday, Companion of our lives,
and, like every day lately, we would like to avoid it.
We cannot seem to find the energy we need,
we cannot bear to turn on the news,
we're even nervous about opening the blinds,
wondering what might be outside.

How shall we pray this morning?

It is Monday, Breath of creation;
so help us to take a moment now to simply sit and
take in a few deep breaths to calm ourselves:
a moment to breathe a little easier
in this strange time …

How shall we pray this morning?

It is Monday, God in Community, Holy and One,
so, could you surprise the folk who feel winter

has been their daily companion
with some warmth and sun?

Could you open our eyes, so that rather than staring
blankly at the horizon,
we might see all the kids
out riding their bikes,
dropping off notes and supplies to neighbours?

Could you give us the energy, the hope, the grace, the wonder
to indeed see this day, this Monday,
as the day you have made, as a gift for us?

May we rejoice in you this day, this Monday. Amen

Benediction:

And now, may the peace of the gentle breezes,
the peace of the singing birds,
the peace of the shining sun,
and the deep, deep peace of the Child of Peace
be with you.
Amen

Evening prayer

Opening:

Softly, gently, lovingly cradle us this night, O God,
that we might sleep soundly until morning. Amen

Song: 'O gladsome light' or 'Holy Spirit, come to us' (Taizé)

Canticle:

As the shadows gather
and twilight creeps across
the lawn, covering the bushes,
I gather up my thoughts
from this day (as well as my worries/fears …),
offering them all to you
as an evening sacrifice.

I cannot enter your house,
but you do gather me into your heart,
where my praise for your enduring love
joins the voices of so many.

There were moments in this day
when I needed to hear
a voice of hope,
a whisper of grace,
just a snippet of peace, and
every time, every time,
there you were, with

just the right words,
the comforting tone.

If they are smart (which
seems in doubt),
the wealthy and powerful
will learn to listen more to you
than to what the ever-changing polls say,
because then they will come to know
the joy songs.
So continue to teach them, God,
until they finally pay attention.

I am (and so is everybody else)
walking in a wilderness
of worries these days;
but you are beside us, protecting us

in the palm of your hands,
the crook of your arm,
the comfort of your lap of hope,
so that everything will come together for the good
you intend for everyone,
in that love which never fades
and is the foundation of all you do.

Prayer:

For what shall we pray this night?

O God, how we long to see your face
in these days of uncertainty and fear!

May we see you in those
boxing up food for all who hunger;
may we see you in people everywhere
who pray and work for neighbours before themselves;
may we see you in the older folk
pressing their hands up against the sides
of a window in a care home.

For what shall we pray this night?

O Jesus, how we long to hear your voice
in these times of worry and wonder!

May we listen for you in the songs
of virtual choirs from all over the world;
may we hear your grace in the comfort
offered by caregivers in hospitals;
may we be filled with the lullabies
whispered by children to their stuffed animals.

For what shall we pray this night?

O Spirit, how we long for your sweet breath
to seep into our lungs, hearts and souls this night!

May it come in the breezes that cool
our feverish fears wrapping around us;
may we feel it in the quiet breathing
of that person, that dog, that cat lying next to us;
may it fill our weary souls with so much hope –
we cannot wait to share it with others tomorrow!

For what shall we pray this night?

O God, let us see your face!
O Jesus, let us hear your voice!
O Spirit, breathe upon us!
This we pray, this night, this very night! Amen

Benediction:

And now, may the peace of the rolling waves,
the peace of the silent mountains,
the peace of the singing stars,
and the deep, deep peace of the Prince of Peace
be with you.
Amen

TUESDAY

Morning prayer

Opening:

In the songs of the birds, may we hear your voice;
in the warmth of the sun, may we feel your grace, O God. Amen

Song: 'Though I may speak' or 'Jesu, tawa pano' (Patrick Matsikenyiri)

Canticle:

I wake up and
life is so heavy
I cannot move, so
please listen to my words,
my heart, my lonely sighs,
my God, my Hope.

I offer you all the longings
of my heart, and wait to see
how you will respond,
but do I notice?
Do I pay attention
to how you want lives
of goodness and grace,

not greed and selfishness;
that you surround yourself
with the compassionate,
not the idolisers, the cruel?
Do I look and see you
turning away from the liars,
the tricksters, the twisters?

Yet, because of that love
of yours which does not give up,
I find the energy to get up,
sit outside in your creation,
listen to the sounds of silence,
offering my heart to you and
following you into those places
where I can offer kindness.

It is tempting, and always easier,
to listen to those whose words
are as hollow as their hearts,
who would deceive people
with easy promises and gifts
they immediately take back.

But you hold them accountable,
sending them back to Grace's school
until they learn your ways of goodness.
And for those who continue
to try to be your children,
even when we mess up,

you continue to homeschool us,
offering online courses in hope,
gathering us into your heart
where we learn the songs of wonder
so we can praise the One
who watches over us, even
when we are too busy to notice.

Prayer:

How shall we pray this morning?

Many of us have had enough, God of our lives,
enough of the isolation within walls closing in on us,
enough of the social distancing which prohibits hugging a friend,
enough of the stay-at-home orders issued by people
who are not in their homes themselves.

So, may we become as wise as health directors,
and as innocent as our neighbours hunkered in their houses.

How shall we pray this morning?

Many of us have had enough, Jesus of our days,
and are ready to get back to life, to living,
to walking around stores browsing,
to crowding into movie theatres and restaurants,
to being able to attend sporting events
with everyone cheering and high-fiving each other.

So, may we become as wise as the CEOs saying, 'No, it is still too early,'
and as innocent as the folk wearing masks everywhere they go.

How shall we pray this morning?

Many of us have had enough, Spirit of wisdom,
and are looking for easy explanations and solutions to this 'new normal',
buying corona cures online that are only sugar water
and believing that the worst is behind us.

So, may we become as wise as the scientists and doctors,
and as innocent as the kids who refuse to go to parties and beaches,
for fear of bringing home the virus to their grandparents.

How shall we pray this morning?

May we be wise enough to use the intelligence you gave us,
God in Community, Holy and One,
and innocent enough to believe that you are with us
in our foolishness, our fears and our future. Amen

Benediction:

And now, may the peace of the gentle breezes,
the peace of the singing birds,
the peace of the shining sun,
and the deep, deep peace of the Child of Peace
be with you.
Amen

Evening prayer

Opening:

Still our souls and quiet our hearts, dear God,
that we may hear your voice of peace. Amen

Song: 'Now, on land and sea descending' or 'Jesus, remember me'

Canticle:

As the sun begins to fade
over the edge of the west
and weariness seeps into my soul,
I know I can find the hope I need
in the comfort of your lap,
as I whisper, 'You are the love
I have longed for; I am nothing
without you.'

I learned this from my mother,
the teachers, the preachers,
the fellow pilgrims who show
me the way, especially when
I can't see it, or want to stay
by the side of the road.

Oh, there are other choices
offered in this world, in these days;
folk who promise so much,
their temptations niggling at my heart,

but I try my best not to listen,
my best not to whisper their names.

Despite what they may say,
I know without a doubt
that you are the One for me.
You place me in a neighbourhood
where justice, grace, hope
are all my neighbours.

At night, now, in these moments,
I can look back over the day
and see where you were,
who you were in,
how you helped me to hold
my life together when I was
ready to fall to pieces, and
I can let your words of love
seep into my soul as I sleep.

So, as I lay my head on the pillow,
and my fears and worries in your hands,
I can sing songs of trust and hope,
knowing that the shadows, the night,
not even death itself, have no power over me,
for you hold us in every moment;
you shine your light so we can see the way;
we can hold on to your hand,
knowing you will never let go.

Prayer:

For what shall we pray this night?

Like a big dog suddenly turning into a quivering
mass of jelly in a storm,
our fears, our worries, our dreads
can shake us to the core of our being,
convincing us that what lies outside
is more powerful than the love, the grace
which you have placed within our hearts.

God of all weathers,
be the thunder vest we need in these days.

For what shall we pray this night?

Like the power-workers warming up their trucks,
slipping on their weather gear, faithfully preparing to go out
to remove fallen trees and restore electricity,
you are willing to take risks to care.

Jesus of those hit hard by the howling gales of life,
be the one we can call when the power
of our hope goes out.

For what shall we pray this night?

Like a cat sitting in a window, watching lightning
brighten the sky,
you teach us to be brave in the face of challenges,
to look for the wonder in everything around us,

to listen for that still, small voice
which follows the storm.

Spirit who rides upon the winds,
be the gentle presence
who purrs to us of hope and life.

For what shall we pray this night?

Like all of creation –
which trusts in your imagination,
which reveals the wonders of your heart,
which plants the seeds of grace, hope and peace –
God in Community, Holy and One,
we will rest safe and secure
in your love this night. Amen

Benediction:

And now, may the peace of the rolling waves,
the peace of the silent mountains,
the peace of the singing stars,
and the deep, deep peace of the Prince of Peace
be with you.
Amen

WEDNESDAY

Morning prayer

Opening:

Splash our souls with living water, tender God,
so we may awake into your joy and wonder. Amen

Song: 'Saviour, like a shepherd lead us' or 'I waited patiently for God' (John L Bell)

Canticle:

We walk on air,
when we refuse to go to
the self-help seminar
hosted by Incorrigibles, Inc;
when we won't put our feet
in the footprints left
by those who trespass
through life;
when we refuse
to sit down in the seats
vacated by the sceptics;

rather,
God tickles us pink
by handing us a credo
which we can chew on
in silence and hope –
until we hunger for nothing else.

Rooted deeply in grace and mercy,
we yield a harvest
in every season of life;
our gifts do not need
to be raked up and taken
to the landfill –
we turn out well.

The reprobates are blown about
like dandelion puffs;
they won't be able
to break in line ahead of us,
or sit in the front row.

God sweeps up the litter
the vandals have thrown
on the sidewalk,
and watches us play
hopscotch all day long.

Prayer:

How shall we pray this morning?

It's another hump day, but then every day, these days, is such a day:
a day to keep weariness from climbing out of bed with us,
a day to push the heavy rock of worry up the hill,
a day to just keep going, until we get past it to tomorrow.

Yet this is the day you made, Creative God,
and so, may we discover how to rejoice in it:
by listening to the dance music of the kid next door
and the new songs of your heart;
by noticing the smiling eyes strangers.

How shall we pray this morning?

It's another day in the wilderness,
and we wonder how in the world we will survive,
when our hair grows longer and our tempers shorter,
when each hour seems like a week,
when we are tempted to give in to the feast of fear the Evil One offers.

Yet this is the day you spoke into being, Jesus of the desert,
and so, may we find the words to say no to the worries
nibbling at our hearts;
no to the seductive words of those who really don't care about us;
no to the longing to stop being safe, and thus endanger everyone.

How shall we pray this morning?

It's another day in the neighbourhood,
and we wonder if we will ever become the people we were
before fear moved into all the houses (including ours),
before we had to shelter in place as if we had no hope,
before we had to isolate ourselves, as if our friends had become zombies.

Yet this is the day you breathe upon us, Spirit of life,
and so, may we notice hope rehabbing the neighbourhood:
delivery folk dropping off unexpected gifts of grace on porches;
love starting to spring up from the once-barren soil of our hearts.

How shall we pray this morning?

Yes, it is just another day, but it is *your* day,
God in Community, Holy and One,
and so, may we open our hearts, our souls, our eyes
and rejoice in it, over and over. Amen

Benediction:

And now, may the peace of the gentle breezes,
the peace of the singing birds,
the peace of the shining sun,
and the deep, deep peace of the Child of Peace
be with you.
Amen

Evening prayer

Opening:

We will lie down to sleep in peace,
knowing that we are not alone
but that you, O God, keep us safe this night. Amen

Song: 'Be not afraid' or 'Wait for the Lord' (Taizé)

Canticle:

Before bedtime, we
sit on the floor and play pat-a-cake
with you, laughing
every time our palms miss,
and especially when you get
that silly look on your face –
and we know you do it
on purpose, you who are
so high and mighty.

Then using your God-voice, you
announce that it is time to head
up to our rooms, and you kneel
down so we can all crawl up
on your back for one last ride
of the day, and we sing lullabies with you
as you slowly go up, step by step.

Giving us one last drink of water,
you tuck us into bed, giving us a kiss;
and shutting the door so that just
a sliver of light shines through,
you sit at the top of the stairs, until we
fall asleep and you can head down
to your home office to keep an eye
on the rest of the worlds.

Prayer:

For what shall we pray this night?

We will lie down this night with you, O God,
and pray you will lie down with us:
the fearful who need a hand to hold,
the weary longing for grace's strength,
the isolated facing more days of solitude,
the workers wondering if their jobs will survive.

For what shall we pray this night?

We will lie down this night with you, O Jesus,
and pray you will lie down with us:
the forgotten who long to be remembered,
the vulnerable living on the edge of life,
the devastated seeking a sense of restoration,
the lonely hoping for someone to contact them.

For what shall we pray this night?

We will lie down this night with you, O Spirit,
and pray you will lie down with us:

the frontline workers wondering if anyone cares,
the aged couple still separated from one another,
the angry and frustrated who hunger for peace,
the toss-and-turners aching for just one night of good sleep.

For what shall we pray this night?

We will lie down this night with you,
God, Jesus, Spirit,
Holy Family who watches over us,
and pray you will lie down with us. Amen

Benediction:

And now, may the peace of the rolling waves,
the peace of the silent mountains,
the peace of the singing stars,
and the deep, deep peace of the Prince of Peace
be with you.
Amen

THURSDAY

Morning prayer

Opening:

Open our eyes to discover your wonder, O God.
Open our lips to praise your name. Amen

Song: 'Take my hand, Precious Lord' or 'The Lord is my song'

Canticle:

Every morning
(having noticed our faces
peering through the fence)
you invite us
to join you in your backyard
called creation, learning new songs
taught by your heart!

The squirrel storing peanuts
even in the summer heat,
the blue jay perched on
the pot filled with rosemary,
the ducklings waddling behind
mum, as she leads them to the pond,

here is where we praise you
in that great sanctuary called the world.

We are blessed when we can
learn the callisthenics of grace
from you, taking a break to drink
from the fountain we thought broken,
and then playing a pickup game of football.

When we are done, you
gather us on the back porch,
handing us big mugs of sugary tea,
asking us to keep an eye
on the veggies (but to let the
bunnies play among the lettuce)
while you go in to set the table
for a great big English breakfast.

Prayer:

How shall we pray this morning?

We are tired, God, of this weary year.

We are tired of going to bed exhausted
and then taking hours to fall asleep,
or falling asleep quickly, only to wake up
at two in the morning
and lying awake.

We are tired of waking up
and dreading to turn on the news

or open the door to grab the newspaper,
knowing how the stories will wear us out.

We don't know if we need more caffeine,
more hope, more grace, more what?,
but we are tired.

How shall we pray this morning?

We are tired, Jesus of the deserted places.

We are tired of not being able to go shopping,
and worn down by our fears of going into a store.

We are tired of having to order everything online,
and exhausted from wondering about the health
and the safety protocols of every delivery person.

We don't know if we need more caffeine,
more hope, more grace, more what?,
but we are tired.

How shall we pray this morning?

We are tired, Spirit of fresh winds and new lives.

We are tired of people sharing foolishness on social media,
and irritated at ourselves for being sucked in by such posts.

We are weary of those who care only for themselves,
even as they proclaim great compassion for the sick and dying.

We are exhausted by this weariness which won't go away,
and worn down to the nubs of our souls by worry.

We don't know if we need more caffeine,
more hope, more grace, more what?,
but we are tired.

How shall we pray this morning?

We don't know if we need more caffeine,
more hope, more grace, more what?,
but we are tired, God in Community, Holy and One,
so just hold us in our weariness, we pray. Amen

Benediction:

And now, may the peace of the gentle breezes,
the peace of the singing birds,
the peace of the shining sun,
and the deep, deep peace of the Child of Peace
be with you.
Amen

Evening prayer

Opening:

Let us crawl up into your lap this night, Parenting God,
as you sing us lullabies of love. Amen

Song: 'O for a world' or 'Nothing can trouble' (Taizé)

Canticle:

Blow the dust off the drums,
put new strings on the banjo,
get the piano tuned,
hand wooden spoons to little kids,
start playing the golden oldies –
while making up new songs for God!

Sit down, play scrabble with God,
forming new words from grace's pile of letters,
words like justice and hope,
words describing stars and sunsets –
and God's incredible language of love:
love as sweet as a crisp apple,
love as tart as summer lemonade,
love as fresh as an autumn breeze,
love that is deeper than our fears.

God knocks over the house of cards
we build from our foolish thoughts,
simply by asking us to hope in the Heart of love,
and to trust as deeply as did

our grandparents in faith.
We are blessed when we trust in God,
when we see each other as a family.

God keeps an eye out for all of us,
watching carefully to see if
we love without reservation,
if we offer compassion without condition,
if leaders turn away from power and threats,
offering justice and grace instead.

The Spirit twirls in joyful circles when we
honour the divine image in others,
when we pick up hope from
the shattered places of life,
when we choose love,
when we feed all who wander through
food and fear deserts.

In moments of grief and pain
beyond imagining, we wait,
and here comes God:
in those who run toward hate to transform it into love;
who shelter little ones from horror.

We trust, and so we hope.
We hope, and so we offer our hearts
to the One who fills them with grace.

Every time we trust, we hope, we come,
God is waiting

every time.

Prayer:

For what shall we pray this night?

Some days, God of our eyes, we can see
all those things which are important to us,
so close we can almost touch them:
our family, our homes, our possessions,
our beliefs, our needs, our desires;

but all those things which are further away –
the family down the street losing everything,
the old folk in the locked-down nursing home,
the people whose political views drive us up a wall –
those all seem so blurry.

So, cure our myopia with those corrective lenses
called compassion and loving our neighbour.

For what shall we pray this night?

Every once in a while, Jesus of horizons,
we can look off into the distance and catch a glimpse
of hope coming our way and we know we just have to be patient;
we can see that proverbial light at the end of the tunnel
and keep moving toward it;
we can see that healthier future all these safety protocols
are pointing us toward,

but then the fellow right next door who has been furloughed
for the last six months,
the mother of the autistic child just across the street,

who has no time to home-school her son,
the retirees in the downstairs apartment who wonder
how they're ever going to pay for their meds and groceries –
all these folk, right at the end of our noses,
appear to us as unfocused blobs.

So, cure our hyperopia with those corrective lenses
ground from hope, kindness and generosity.

For what shall we pray this night?

Operate on us like a laser, Spirit of our lives:
so we are able to read the fine print about forgiveness,
service and caring that is found in the good news,
and have vision.

For what shall we pray this night?

By your grace and love,
to see ourselves, our neighbours, our friends
and those strangers who are our sisters and brothers,
through your eyes,
God in Community, Holy and One. Amen

Benediction:

And now, may the peace of the rolling waves,
the peace of the silent mountains,
the peace of the singing stars,
and the deep, deep peace of the Prince of Peace
be with you.
Amen

FRIDAY

Morning prayer

Opening:

As the sun rises this day to warm creation,
may we know the depth of your love, O God. Amen

Song: 'Womb of life, and source of being' or 'Ubi caritas' (Taizé)

Canticle:

Sing with joy!
From the farthest galaxies,
to little kids in bathtubs.

Sing with joy, stars and planets,
and you astronauts at the space station.

From the meadows, let horses neigh,
from the ocean depths, let dolphins whistle,
let raindrops beat a pattern on tin roofs
and brittle ice crack like cymbals;
let bighorn sheep bleat out notes
and trees do liturgical dance on the hills.

Panthers roaring from tree branches
and kittens mewling behind their mothers;
puppies thumping their tails on kitchen floors –
all sing with joy!

Big shots, not-so-hots, has-beens
and hopes-to-be, people in line
for advancements and furloughed workers,
little tykes, young turks, classic citizens –
all join to sing with joy!

Lifting God's name to the stars,
the name all creation knows:

Glory Rider through the universes,
Trumpet Player in Trinity's band,
the One folk push closer to in order
to hear the sweet notes
of joy and wonder,
grace and hope.

Sing with joy, all God's children!

Prayer:

How shall we pray this morning?

It's Friday, Day Maker, and oh, how we used
to look forward to this day – the end of the work week and
the beginning of the weekend;
but now it is just another day in a long string of days,
a string that, as it stretches out, becomes tauter and tauter.

So, open our eyes to the wonder we overlook in our weariness;
take our worries out of our ears
so we can hear the morning songs of birds;
crack open our locked hearts
so we might share love with others.

How shall we pray this morning?

It's Friday, Lord of all time, and once we would be making plans
to get together with friends after work for happy hour,
or to take our love out on the town, maybe on a first date;
we'd be thinking about what movies to go and see,
what art gallery to explore …
But now it's just another day
with endless hours that stretch out.

So, remind us that happy hour is now,
when we can FaceTime with friends,
when we can pick out a movie that the kids want to watch
and eat popcorn together,
when we can discover delight in exploring galleries and museums
halfway around the world,
all by way of the gift of technology.

How shall we pray this morning?

It's Friday, Spirit of every moment, and in another life
we'd be glancing at the clock,
counting down the minutes till we could punch out
and be free.

But now the clock is something we avoid;
now we count the minutes in every hour.

So, give us the grace to fill our minutes
with kindness to others;
help us to use these hours to write notes to friends,
or better yet, call them;
show us how to use our time
making masks,
praying for doctors and nurses,
volunteering at the food pantry,
offering a listening ear to a lonely neighbour …

How shall we pray this morning?

It's Friday, Day Maker, Lord of all time, Spirit of every moment.
Remind us that we still have reason to thank you for it. Amen

Benediction:

And now, may the peace of the gentle breezes,
the peace of the singing birds,
the peace of the shining sun,
and the deep, deep peace of the Child of Peace
be with you.
Amen

Evening prayer

Opening:

As we lay our weary souls down to rest this night,
come and watch over us, O God. Amen

Song: 'I heard the voice of Jesus say' or 'Our darkness is never darkness in your sight' (Taizé)

Canticle:

Glancing around the dinner table,
God asks, once again:

'How long will you keep messing up?
Why do you keep siding with injustice
and keep doing the bidding of the cruel?
Justice is the gift you offer
to the forgotten, the vulnerable;
speak out and stand up
for the ones ignored by the powerful.
Release the grip of the hateful
on children and families, and
welcome them into your hearts.'

Although we have all sorts
of degrees on our walls, we
are dumber than dirt.

God reminds us, 'You are not me,

and time is running out on
your arrogant grasping for holiness.'

Come, O Lord,
with justice and mercy
for every corner of life.

Prayer:

For what shall we pray this night?

We pray, God our Parent, that your grace might rest upon us:
like an afghan knitted by our favourite uncle,
like a quilt sewn by a neighbour's daughter,
like a blanket worn and frayed from keeping
children and grandchildren warm over the years.

For what shall we pray this night?

We pray, Jesus our brother, that your hope might be over us:
sheltering us from the worries swirling around,
forming a tent in which we can hide and read a book by flashlight,
being an umbrella to keep the storms of doubt
from soaking us to the very marrow of our souls.

For what shall we pray this night?

We pray, our soulmate Spirit, that your peace might be under us:
like a deep mattress to cradle our weary bodies,
like slippers to warm our feet on frosty mornings,
like a grandmother's lap in which we can fall asleep gently,
like a soft lawn on which we can stretch out
and gaze up at the stars.

104 How shall we pray this morning? For what shall we pray this night?

For what shall we pray this night?

We pray for your peace, your hope, your grace
to always be with us, as you are in every moment,
God in Community, Holy and One. Amen

Benediction:

And now, may the peace of the rolling waves,
the peace of the silent mountains,
the peace of the singing stars,
and the deep, deep peace of the Prince of Peace
be with you.
Amen

SATURDAY

Morning prayer

Opening:

Listen to our prayers this day, O God.
Hear the cries of our pleading. Amen

Song: 'God is calling through the whisper' or 'Sing, praise and bless the Lord' (Taizé)

Canticle:

When you receive the latest
huff-and-puff from me,
be kind
and hit the delete button.

When I spend each moment
hanging out with the wrong crowd,
be patient
and send truth to be
my best friend.

When I wallow
in the muddy mess of me,
put me in the machine,

the unmentionables
on a gentle setting,
and let me dry in
peace's sweet breath.

When I hear the bell
on sin's seductive ice-cream van
coming down the street,
be quick
to turn up the boom box
playing the glad choruses
of your heart.

When you could
toss me out with
the rest of the junk,
be an old softie,
cradling me in your heart,
tenderly polishing me
with your scarred hands,
until I reflect
the hopeful gleam
in your eye.

Then, I will share
my transformation
on a Zoom meeting,
asking everyone
to turn up the volume
so together we can sing

songs of joy, before
heading out the door
to care for all those
who bounce on the
trampoline with fear,
who arm-wrestle with loneliness,
who need someone to bring
the glue of grace to help them
put their lives back together.

And when we do, we
will create communities
which are filled with
laughter, justice, kindness, love,
just as you hope.

Prayer:

How shall we pray this morning?

It's Saturday, O God, when we like to sleep in
and snuggle under the covers with the one we love,
but we woke up early again, stress whispering in our ears:
'Get up, sleepyheads, I've got a busy busy day planned.'

So, help us instead to discover your Saturday, God of hope:
filled with the wonder of creation we are usually too busy to notice,
filled with quiet moments of just sitting and listening and being,
filled with the gentle touch of those checking up on us.

How shall we pray this morning?

It's Saturday, Lord of our lives, and we would now usually be
heading out the door to the games of kids and grandkids,
to sit on the sidelines with other adults barely awake.
But now we are all sidelined; and to be honest,
if we have to watch one more rerun
of one more decades-old sporting event,
we will throw the TV across the room.

So, help us to discover your Saturday, Jesus of fun and games:
as we rediscover 'the thrill of victory and agony of defeat' in Scrabble,
as we challenge everyone to a winner-take-all game of tiddlywinks,
as we let our little ones create silly games with rules made up as we go.

How shall we pray this morning?

It's Saturday, Spirit of the day, and we might be getting ready
to head out to the nursery to buy some plants;
but wonder now if we might pick up more than just flowers
if we go into the store, and so figure we might instead
just sit and watch the grass and dandelions grow.

So, help us to discover your Saturday, Spirit of gentleness:
as we open up the book we got for Christmas but haven't touched,
as we lounge out on the patio with a cup of tea and just rest,
as we pull on our well-worn shoes and head out for our daily walk.

How shall we pray this morning?

It's Saturday, God, Jesus, Spirit, another not-as-usual Saturday,
so, help us to discover your Saturday of wonder,
hope and gentleness. Amen

Benediction:

And now, may the peace of the gentle breezes,
the peace of the singing birds,
the peace of the shining sun,
and the deep, deep peace of the Child of Peace
be with you.
Amen

Evening prayer

Opening:

O God, you are the One who keeps us safe.
You wrap us in love in every moment.
Be with us now, we pray. Amen

Song: 'When twilight comes' or 'Kum ba yah'

Canticle:

Lord, can you hear me?
You might have to lean
way over, since I am down here
in this hole I dug with
the shovel fear gave me.

I thought you wouldn't
be able to find me or
my foolishness but
then you dropped that note
down to me, reading 'It's
okay. You're all right in my book.'

So now, sitting on the edge
after Spirit pulled me out,
I will just wait,
kicking my heels,
singing songs to myself.

Hope is that heirloom
passed down to us by
our grandparents in the faith,
who knew that you alone
can rescue us; you alone
can pull us out of every hole
we dig.

Prayer:

For what shall we pray this night?

They keep showing up during the day,
God who watches over us, those fears
that are such a part of our lives.
One pops up while we are watching the news,
and no matter how quickly we push it down,
another raises its head with the next story.

A fear shows up when we see unmasked folk
wandering the grocery stores,
or walking into a restaurant,
or standing in line at the post office.

So many fears popping up,
we feel like we've played a game of whack-a-mole
by the time evening comes around.

For what shall we pray this night?

We really long to be on the side of justice,
Jesus who watches over the vulnerable,

to bring hope and healing to communities
and those close to us.

But with all the distractions from politicians,
and all the defensive comments by 'experts',
we're like Mario and Luigi in the computer game,
trying to get past all the side-scrolling stages,
seeking to rescue our sisters and brothers
from hate and indifference.

For what shall we pray this night?

We struggle to be people of peace,
Spirit of life, grace and community,
to walk with those whose dreams have been deferred
and whose hopes have been denied.

But we feel like we have to spend so much time
trying to dodge all the barrels filled with bitterness,
or with the twisted history taught to so many,
or with the stale lies told so often that they become 'truth',
that Cranky Kong keeps rolling our way.

For what shall we pray this night?

As we seek to be people of peace,
to be found on the side of justice
and to continue to resist our fears,
may we remember that life is not a game,
but the calling we have been given as your people,
God in Community, Holy and One. Amen

Benediction:

And now, may the peace of the rolling waves,
the peace of the silent mountains,
the peace of the singing stars,
and the deep, deep peace of the Prince of Peace
be with you.
Amen

SUNDAY

Morning prayer

Opening:

O God, fill our hearts and mouths with words of praise,
so that we may offer our thanksgiving to you in these moments. Amen

Song: 'Source and sovereign, rock and cloud' or 'We will meet' (John L Bell and Hans-Olav Moerk)

Canticle:

Oh my gosh!
even in the silence of
empty sanctuaries, echoes
of hallelujah resound!
And out in the empty streets,
the parklands and schoolyards,
the forests, meadows and mountains,
still hallelujahs are heard.

Oh my gosh!
the clouds scudding
across the skies, the
sun playing peekaboo,

the cardinals and robins
balancing on trees, all
sing hallelujahs to God.

So,
let us join them:
blow the dust off
the trumpet and put
new strings on the guitar,
hand some pot-lids
to the kids and tell them
to clang away;
play the spoons,
pound the bongos,
tickle the ivories,
sing off-key.

Oh my gosh!
let's keep shouting
hallelujah to our God.

Oh my gosh!

Prayer:

How shall we pray this morning?

It's Sunday, God of our longings, and if our routines
were not so disrupted, we would be getting ready
to head out to worship in great overflowing churches,
in small country chapels, or in homes,
gathering with our friends, neighbours, even strangers.

But we can't (or shouldn't).
So, as we linger over a late breakfast, read the paper,
watch the news, figure out how to access an online church service,
remind us that, even in our isolation, we are not alone:
we are still a part of your people, because we are your people.

How shall we pray this morning?

It's Sunday, Jesus of our loneliness, and if things were different,
we would be pulling on our Sunday best
and hurrying the slowpokes among us.
As we sit around in our jammies,
looking at the church bulletin e-mailed to us, the online liturgy,
and trying to find the Bible passages for the day,
gather us as your scattered sisters and brothers,
who still are part of the household of faith,
who still long to care for others, even at a distance.

How shall we pray this morning?

It's Sunday, Breath of Creation, and rather than being inside somewhere,
we have a chance to do what so many folk say
is just as good as being in a church: worship God in nature.

So, even if we are stuck inside, may we notice the sky,
the trees, the birds, the critters, the leaves moving in the breeze.
Though we are no Wendell Berrys, may we go out and find you
in the cathedrals of forests, in the sanctuaries of local parks,
in the little country churches of our backyards,
praying for the gift of creation, for the breath of life,
for the wonder of this day, for your steadfast love.

How shall we pray this morning?

It's Sunday, God in Community, Holy and One,
and we offer our hearts, our lives, our souls
in worship to you, as always. Amen

Benediction:

And now, may the peace of the gentle breezes,
the peace of the singing birds,
the peace of the shining sun,
and the deep, deep peace of the Child of Peace
be with you.
Amen

Evening prayer

Opening:

O God, come to us in the shadows of our lives.
O God, be quick to make yourself known to us. Amen

Song: 'Like the murmur of the dove's song' or 'Nunc dimittis' (Taizé)

Canticle:

Sometimes
I just want to crawl up
in your lap and have you
wrap your arms around me,
or curl up under the covers
with you, where you listen
to our broken hearts.

A haven,
a cradle,
a hiding place,
that is what we need sometimes.

Just like all those
around us, the ones
who are bullied by the cruel,
who are mistreated
by those who worship hate.
You seek to protect them

(and us) in these moments
when everything is crumbling,
when everyone is grumbling,
where everyone is angry,
where no one is listening.

You love us
pure and simple,
as purely and simply as
a parent loves their child.

You listen to us,
you pick us up,
you heal us,
you grace us,

and so, we love you,
simply, purely, hopefully.

Prayer:

For what shall we pray this night?

Surely, we must pray laments this night,
God of the broken and of the frightened.

Laments for those who have lost their lives
from violence, from fear, from hate,
as well as for those whose lives
are filled with violence, with fear, with hate.

Laments for those who have lived in the shadows
of despair, of poverty, of prejudice,
as well as for those whose wealth, whose privilege
blinds them to the sufferings of other human beings.

Lord, hear our prayers …

For what shall we pray this night?

Surely, we must pray for justice this night,
Jesus of the forgotten, of the ostracised.

Justice for those who see all the cards
stacked against them,
as well as for those who deal the cards.

Justice for those whose care, whose housing,
whose medical coverage become pawns
in the game we call politics,
as well as for those who make up all the rules,
and change them whenever they want.

Lord, hear our prayers …

For what shall we pray this night?

Surely, we must pray for peace this night,
Spirit of compassion, Spirit of grace.

Peace for communities which have seen
livelihoods destroyed, neighbourhoods terrorised,
as well as for peace for those who will get up
tomorrow and sweep, paint, rebuild their communities.

Peace for folk who have known no peace,
no hope, no future, no chances all their lives,
as well as for those who live in peace, whose hope
is abundant, whose future is secured,
who never have to leave anything to chance.

Lord, hear our prayers …

For what shall we pray this night?

Surely, and simply, we lament those chances
we had to make a difference, but did not.

Surely, and simply, we pray for justice:
to bring an end to racism, to hatred,
to indifference, to cruelty,
to treating others less than ourselves.

Surely, and simply, we pray for peace:
the peace that can freely walk our streets,
the peace that can rebuild our hopes,
the peace that can make us your people,
God in Community, Holy and One. Amen

Benediction:

And now, may the peace of the rolling waves,
the peace of the silent mountains,
the peace of the singing stars,
and the deep, deep peace of the Prince of Peace
be with you.
Amen

Bible readings and poems for two weeks

First week

Day 1

For wisdom, the fashioner of all things, taught me.
Wisdom of Solomon 7:22a (NRSV)

You put down the hammer and saw,
you step away from the loom,
you lay aside the quilting squares
to gather us on
your lap to trace the words;
with your fingers
we begin to learn how to
read the faces of others,
to listen to the whispers of their souls,
to hold their wounded hearts in ours,
to freely give away all the
grace, hope, peace and joy
you share with us every moment.

Day 2

He makes me lie down in green pastures;
he leads me beside still waters;
    he restores my soul.
He leads me in right paths
    for his name's sake.

Psalm 23:2–3 (NRSV)

God,
grant me the
serenity
to take breaks
from the Internet,

the courage
to ignore the trolls
on social media,

and the
wisdom
to come in
from the
Twitterstorms.

Day 3

He said to them, 'But who do you say that I am?'
Luke 9:20a (NRSV)

You are
the brokenness
that makes us whole.

The weakness
that gives us strength.

The foolishness
that makes us aware.

The emptiness
that fills our hollow souls.

The One
who makes us family.

Day 4

In the thirtieth year, in the fourth month, on the fifth day of the month, as I was among the exiles by the river Chebar, the heavens were opened, and I saw visions of God.
Ezekiel 1:1 (NRSV)

Through those years
of loneliness,
those months of
utter fear,
those days of despair
which never seem to end,
help us to see
your joy in the little
child jumping in puddles,
your wonder in stars
shimmering in night skies,
your arms in the hope
which cradles us
for as long as we need.

Day 5

The beginning of the good news of Jesus Christ, the Son of God.
Mark 1:1 (NRSV)

May grace
be as fresh
as a lover's kiss.

May hope
awaken in our hearts
each morning.

May peace
be the whisper
that challenges
our apathy.

May the gospel
never become as stale
as the bread
we left out
on the counter
last night.

Day 6

The whole assembly kept silence, and listened to Barnabas and Paul as they told of all the signs and wonders that God had done through them among the Gentiles.
Acts 15:12 (NRSV)

In the silence,
may we hear the
voices of humility,
instead of our own
filled with arrogance.

In the silence,
let us listen
to the chatter of kids
of the wonders they find
in their backyards.

In the silence,
whisper to us
of the signs we might
hear, see, taste, touch,
if we just spent more
of our lives

in the silence.

Day 7

Do not hide your face from me
  in the day of my distress.
Psalm 102:2a (NRSV)

In these days
of uncertainty,
of fears nipping
at our heels and
worries stalking us,
may we see you
in the faces
of chalk-drawing kids,
mask-sewing neighbours,
weary night-nurses,
and friends caring
for the strangers they meet.

Second week

Day 1

So too at the present time there is a remnant, chosen by grace.
Romans 11:5

They may have the podium
with all the microphones,
but we will still
speak of justice.

They may seduce folk
with bitter words,
but we will still
embrace everyone.

They may be certain
that they will always
be powerful,
but we will still
serve in weakness.

They may be convinced
we are outnumbered,
but we will still
be sharers of grace.

Day 2

It is the Lord who goes before you. He will be with you; he will not fail you or forsake you. Do not fear or be dismayed.
Deuteronomy 31:8 (NRSV)

Wondering how we
made it past yesterday,
we only need to look back
to see you picking up
the litter of our fears
we left by the side of the road.

Worried as to how we
will ever reach the end
of this long, weary day,
we only need to glance
ahead of us, to see you
filling in the potholes
of our loneliness, so
we will not trip and fall,

and so, we know that
tomorrow can hold no
terror for us, for you
are already there,
waiting for us
to catch up.

Day 3

What then are we to say about these things?
Romans 8:31a (NRSV)

Simply this:

God
has not forsaken us
has not forgotten us
has not walked away from us.

God
has a tight grip on us
has wrapped us in love
pours grace into our souls

for

neither foolish politicians
nor those who make bad choices,

neither a virus we cannot see
nor the angry we can hear,

neither what yesterday, today
nor tomorrow bring, nothing,
absolutely not a thing (!),

will ever, will ever, will ever
separate us from the love of
God.

Day 4

If anyone says anything to you, just say this, 'The Lord needs them.'
Matthew 21:3a (NRSV)

When you wear a mask
and someone gives
you grief about it,
tell them it is what
Jesus needs you to do.

When people mock you
for standing six metres
(or more) from others,
remind them it is what
Jesus hopes we will do.

If people believe you are silly
to care so much about
others instead of your 'rights',
simply ask them
if they think Jesus needs
them to be so callous.

Day 5

Lord, you have been our dwelling place
    in all generations.
Psalm 90:1(NRSV)

When we needed
a heart, you broke
yours for us,

when we needed
a place to rest, you
slept on the floor,
giving us the big
soft feather bed,

when we needed
grace, you decanted
the best year and
poured us a cup,

when we need
anything, you
give us everything.

Day 6

O God, you are my God, I seek you,
    my soul thirsts for you;
my flesh faints for you,
    as in a dry and weary land where there is no water.
Psalm 63:1 (NRSV)

We act as if
getting grace and love
from you
is like trying to get
water from a rusted
hand-pump on dry farmland,
when in fact
you are a
deep spring
and your heart
can never be shut off –

really!

Day 7

The light shines in the darkness, and the darkness did not overcome it.
John 1:5 (NRSV)

Even
in the deepest
shadows,

in the tunnel
no longer used
except by bats,

in the alleys
mouldy with fears,

the tiniest dot of

hope

appears and burns

brighter and brighter

until it illuminates

the way.

Sources and acknowledgements

Passages from NRSV copyright 1989, Division of Christian Education of the National Council of the Churches of Christ in the United States of America. Used by permission. All rights reserved.

Wild Goose Publications, the publishing house of the Iona Community established in the Celtic Christian tradition of Saint Columba, produces books, e-books, CDs and digital downloads on:

- holistic spirituality
- social justice
- political and peace issues
- healing
- innovative approaches to worship
- song in worship, including the work of the Wild Goose Resource Group
- material for meditation and reflection

For more information:

Wild Goose Publications
The Iona Community
21 Carlton Court, Glasgow, G5 9JP, UK

Tel. +44 (0)141 429 7281
e-mail: admin@ionabooks.com

or visit our website at
www.ionabooks.com
for details of all our products and online sales